Diderot : french philosopher
and father of the
Author: Stark, Sam.
Reading Level: 8.1 MG
Point Value: 2.0
ACCELERATED READER QUIZ 100537

DIDEROT

FRENCH PHILOSOPHER AND FATHER OF THE ENCYCLOPEDIA

PHILOSOPHERS OF
THE ENLIGHTENMENT™

DIDEROT

FRENCH PHILOSOPHER AND FATHER OF THE ENCYCLOPEDIA

Sam Stark

rosen
central™

The Rosen Publishing Group, Inc., New York

To Mom and Pop, for teaching me to read

Published in 2006 by The Rosen Publishing Group, Inc.
29 East 21st Street, New York, NY 10010

First Edition

Library of Congress Cataloging-in-Publication Data

Stark, Sam.
Diderot: french philosopher and father of the encyclopedia/
Sam Stark.—1st ed.
    p. cm.—(Philosophers of the Enlightenment)
Includes bibliographical references.
ISBN 1-4042-0418-0 (library binding)
1. Diderot, Denis, 1713–1784. 2. Authors, French—18th century—
Biography. 3. Philosophers—France—Biography. 4. France—Intellectual
life—18th century. 5. Enlightenment—France.
I. Title. II. Series.
PQ1979.S68 2006
034'.1'092—dc22
2004026084

2004026084

Manufactured in Malaysia

On the cover: Background: View of the church of the Sorbonne circa 1825. Inset: A nineteenth-century portrait of Diderot by Dmitri Levitsky.

CONTENTS

SCIENCE AND THE ENLIGHTENMENT

- Leading academic centers
- □ Observatories

Uppsala

Stockholm

SCOTLAND
Smith
Watt
Glasgow

Edinburgh

Copenhagen

Königsberg
Kant

□ Danzig

ENGLAND
Bacon
Boyle
Hume
Locke
Newton

Cambridge

Halle
Berlin

Torun
Copernicus

London
Amsterdam
Van Leeuwenhoek
Spinoza

Göttingen
Leipzig
Leibniz

Greenwich □

Paris
Descartes
Diderot
Montesquieu
Rousseau
Voltaire

Strasbourg

Padua
Galileo
Venice

Turin

Bologna

Madrid

Rome

Naples

0   250   500
MILES

This map shows the leading scientific and academic centers of eighteenth-century Europe. This period of history is known as the Enlightenment. During this period, many important scientific discoveries were made, and new, influential ideas about politics and government spread across all of Europe.

INTRODUCTION

On June 28, 1751, in France, the first volume of a new encyclopedia was published. By today's standards, this encyclopedia was not so large—it was only half as big as the 2004 Encyclopædia Britannica. Neither was it the most reliable book ever written. Many articles contained errors. Others included authors' opinions rather than facts. Some articles were too short, others too long. Some were plagiarized from other reference works, and a few appeared to be put in for fun—they didn't have any useful information at all.

Not only did the contents seem a bit mixed-up and at times wrong, even the title was odd. It was called *Encyclopedia, or Reasoned Dictionary of the Sciences, Arts, and Crafts.* Which was it—an encyclopedia or a

Denis Diderot (1713–1784) is portrayed writing a letter in this 1767 painting. Diderot is best known for his work as the editor of one of the most influential books of the eighteenth century. The book was entitled *Encyclopedia*, which means "circle of knowledge." Consisting of twenty-eight volumes of text and illustrations, it aimed to educate and instruct people in a wide variety of topics. Some of the material in the *Encyclopedia* proved to be controversial, leading it to be banned by the king of France after only seven volumes had been published. However, Diderot continued to work on the project in secrecy until it was completed.

dictionary? Or was it a "reasoned dictionary," whatever that might be?

To understand this unique reference book, we can look at the lives and times of the men behind it. Its authors and editors included some of the most brilliant men of the time. Although these men had their differences, they were united by a belief that the best society is one in which all people are free to discuss ideas and to form their own opinions. The *Encyclopedia* was designed to help people do that. It presented difficult subjects such as history, philosophy, economics, politics, art, and industry in clear and simple language. Although it was not the first reference work to collect facts on a wide variety of subjects, the *Encyclopedia* was unique in its commitment to free thought and free speech for everyone.

The *Encyclopedia* was too large for one person to do alone. Even with dozens working together as a team, it took twenty years to complete. Nonetheless, one man stands out as the driving force behind its creation. That man is Denis Diderot, the main editor of the *Encyclopedia*. Diderot held strong beliefs and ambitions. Some of his beliefs would get him into serious trouble—even land him in jail. Strange as it may sound, the seemingly boring job of creating a massive reference work like the *Encyclopedia* was, in its time and place, quite an adventure.

FREE THINKING IN THE ANCIEN RÉGIME

CHAPTER 1

The *Encyclopedia* was published during the period of French history known as the ancien régime. This period began in 1651, when King Louis XIV came of age. It ended quite suddenly with the French Revolution in 1789. To understand the *Encyclopedia*, we need to know more about life during the ancien régime.

The society of the ancien régime was structured like a pyramid. At the top was the king. Just below the king were three large groups known as estates. The first estate was the clergy, which consisted of members of the church, such as priests and monks. The second estate was the nobility: the dukes and duchesses, barons, and others of noble birth. People who belonged to the first or the second

King Louis XIV (1638–1715) poses in a wig and royal costume in this painting from 1701. Louis was the king of France for seventy-two years (1643–1715), the longest reign of any French monarch. During his reign, Louis expanded France's borders and led the country to new heights in art and culture. The flowerlike pattern on his clothing and in the background is the fleur-de-lis (lily flower). The fleur-de-lis served as a symbol of the French monarchy for many centuries.

THE AGE OF ENLIGHTENMENT

The Enlightenment spanned the eighteenth century in Europe. It was an era in which people's perceptions of their place in the universe changed dramatically. During the Enlightenment, philosophers argued that the creative qualities of humankind were the most important qualities. This creativity was demonstrated by people's ability to reason. Because of this, the Enlightenment is sometimes known as the Age of Reason.

By applying reason, Enlightenment thinkers made important discoveries in science and technology. Also important, enlightenment thinkers encouraged the ideals that remain the goal of many of today's societies. When we speak of such things as liberty, equality, and the pursuit of happiness, we are referring to ideas that became popular during the Enlightenment.

estate had special privileges. For instance, they did not have to pay taxes. Very few people were so lucky. Most people belonged to the third estate. The wealthier part of the third estate was called the bourgeoisie, which is French for "city people."

Doctors, lawyers, businesspeople, shopkeepers, and merchants were in this group. But the majority of the third estate, making up the broad base of the pyramid, were peasants.

THE PALACE OF VERSAILLES

Life at the top of the pyramid of the ancien régime was glamorous. Louis XIV was called the Sun King because the world seemed to revolve around him the way Earth orbits the sun. He built one of the most magnificent palaces in history. The Palace of Versailles expressed his belief that all of France was one big household and he was the father.

The palace could hold almost 10,000 people when it was filled to capacity. Louis XIV received visitors on Mondays, Wednesdays, and Thursdays of each week. On those days the court was crowded with nobility trying to impress one another and catch the eye of the king. Some sense of the glamour of the court of the Sun King is found in the Duchess of Orléans's description of her visit to the palace, as it appears in Frantz Funck-Brentano's book *The Old Regime in France*:

There was such a crowd that one had to wait a quarter of an hour at each door before being able to enter, and I was wearing a dress

Pictured above are two views of the Palace of Versailles. The palace was originally a hunting lodge built by Louis XIV's father. Over a period of fifty years, Louis XIV expanded the lodge into an immense and magnificent complex that became the home of the French monarchy. Today, the palace still stands and is visited by millions of tourists every year. It is located in the city of Versailles, about ten miles (sixteen kilometers) outside of Paris.

and underskirt so horribly heavy that I could hardly stand upright. My costume was of gold trimmed with black chenille flowers, and I had on my pearls and diamonds. My husband was wearing a black velvet coat embroidered with gold, and had on all his large diamonds. My son had a coat embroidered with gold and different colors overlaid with gems. My daughter wore a robe of green velvet embroidered with gold, the dress and underskirt, as well as the corsage, garnished all over with rubies and diamonds.

Needless to say, life at the bottom of the pyramid was quite different from the glamorous life at Versailles. The peasants worked in the fields from dawn to dusk. They had to pay taxes to the king and tithes to the clergy. If they did not own their own land, they also had to pay rent. When all the taxes, rent, and tithes were paid, most peasants had little money left. Very few could afford to buy meat. Most of them lived on a poor diet of cabbage, watery soup, and lots and lots of bread. In fact, the average French peasant ate more than 2 pounds (0.9 kilograms) of bread a day. In many ways, the society that Diderot was born into was still in the Middle Ages.

This painting from 1642 is entitled *The Peasants' Meal*. The painting shows the style of dress and appearance of French peasants during the early reign of Louis XIV. The painting uses dark colors and has a somber tone, which is meant to illustrate the hardship and difficult lives of the peasants. Throughout the seventeenth and eighteenth centuries, peasants made up the majority of the French population.

DEATH OF THE SUN KING

The Sun King died on September 1, 1715. Since his rightful heir was only five years old, a nobleman named Philippe II, the Duke of Orléans, was appointed to run the government until the king came of age.

Under Philippe, and then under Louis XV, politics were different from the way they had been under the Sun King. The nobles, the clergy, and the bourgeoisie had more freedom and power than they had earlier. With this new freedom, the upper classes began to meet at each other's houses, instead of at the palace.

LIFE IN THE SALONS

These upper-class get-togethers were called salons. The word meant something very different in eighteenth-century France from what it means today. The eighteenth-century salon was not a place to get your hair done. Rather, like the old visiting days at Versailles, the salons were an opportunity for nobles and other important people to meet, talk, and mingle. The salons were usually run by wealthy women who selected their guests carefully to ensure that everyone got along.

But the spirit of the salons was somewhat more relaxed than the court at Versailles, which most had found tiresome. People shared ideas and told stories rather than just try to impress one another with their clothes. To be sure, the salons had their share of scandalous rumors and petty personal squabbles, but they were also a place to meet interesting people and share ideas and news. During a time when everything that was published was carefully censored, the salons provided a small oasis of free thinking and free speech.

The wealthy citizens of France, and respected writers and artists gathered at salons. The salon was a very fashionable event, and how people dressed was important, but more important was the conversation and serious discussion of art, literature, and politics. Paris was especially well-known for its salons. Many of these salons were hosted by women. Madame d'Epinay, Julie de Lespinasse, and Madame Helvétius were just a few of the hostesses who became famous for their salons.

The salons were exclusive affairs. Only wealthy people and famous writers or artists were invited. Everyday people had to gather elsewhere. In big cities like Paris, cafés were like salons—places to see and be seen, and where some greater freedom of speech was possible. Unlike salons, these cafés were open to almost everyone, rich or poor. The theaters were also good meeting places. Unlike today, where people sit silently in the dark as they watch movies or plays, the theaters of the ancien régime were social places. People came as much to talk as to watch what was on the stage. In addition to cafés and theaters, there were also areas in the parks where people went to share news and rumors.

These gathering places—salons, cafés, theaters, and even parks—were important places to hear the latest news, partially because books and newspapers were much more rare and expensive than they are today. A newspaper subscription was a luxury, and three-quarters of Parisians owned no books at all. But, more important, they were places outside the influence of the king where people could speak more freely. It was in such places that the *Encyclopedia* was born.

DIDEROT'S YOUTH

Denis Diderot was born on October 5, 1713, in Langres, France. Langres is a small town in the Champagne region, which is famous for its sparkling wine. But the little town of Langres is better known for making cutlery, such as knives and forks, scissors, and other sharp instruments.

In the beginning of the eighteenth century, there were very few factories. Items such as knives were made by hand by experts known as artisans. Becoming an artisan required years of training and hands-on experience. Often a father would teach the secrets of the trade to his son. A young man could also train as an apprentice in a shop.

Didier Diderot, Denis's father, was a master cutler, as his father had been before him. In fact, Diderots had made cutlery in Langres for 200 years.

Denis Diderot was born in Langres, France, and lived there for the first fifteen years of his life. Langres is pictured above in a carving from the eighteenth century. The city is located on the upper Marne River in eastern France. It was built on a limestone bluff to keep it safe from enemy forces. Parts of the stone wall that can be seen in this carving still stand today.

"Diderot" was a trusted brand name. Didier Diderot was particularly known among surgeons for the unusually fine scalpels he made.

The Diderot family was large. Denis's grandmother had twenty-two children! Denis himself had five younger siblings: four sisters and a brother. Two of his sisters died as children. Denis's two surviving younger sisters were named Angélique and Denise. His younger brother was named after his father, Didier.

Denis's favorite sibling was his second sister, Denise, who was smart, kind, and free-spirited. Denis and Denise were close throughout their lives.

The brothers, however, were never very close. His brother was a very religious and serious young man, which was the opposite of Denis's personality. Denis was not very close to Angélique, either, who was also the serious type and became a nun.

THE REBEL

As for Denis Diderot himself, he was an unruly and rebellious child who was always flirting with girls and getting into fights. Here is his description of himself in grammar school, as it appears in Arthur M. Wilson's famous biography of Diderot:

> I was pleasing—pleasing to even the women and girls of my home town . . . They preferred me, without a hat and with chest uncovered, sometimes without shoes, in a jacket and with feet bare, me, son of a worker at a forge, to that little well-dressed

Denise Diderot was a younger sister of Denis's. Besides nearly sharing the same name, they also shared a similar personality. Historian John Morley writes that Diderot described her as being "lively, active, cheerful . . . free in her ways, still more free in her talk . . . the most original and the most strongly-marked creature I know; she is goodness itself."

monsieur, all curled and powdered and dressed to the nines, the son of the presiding judge of the bailiwick court . . . [I was] a boy who revealed his soul by frank and open words and who knew better how to give a blow with his fist than how to make a bow, pleased them more than a foolish, cowardly, false, and effeminate little toady.

Diderot's tough style was not always appreciated by his teachers. His school was run by Jesuit priests, who were very strict. To keep all of the students in line, the priests organized their schools on the model of the Roman army. Diderot didn't take well to such discipline. He was suspended more than once for fighting.

At the same time, Diderot was no thug. He was extraordinarily smart and won prizes in every subject. He did especially well in Latin and math, two subjects that would come in handy later in his life.

Despite his success, at times Diderot struggled to stay interested in school. Once, according to family legend, Diderot asked his father if he could drop out of school and learn the family trade of making cutlery. The experiment only lasted a few days. Diderot made a mess of everything he touched, so he returned to school.

Because he was such a clever boy, Diderot was expected to enter one of the learned professions— doctor, lawyer, or priest. The idea of performing surgery frightened him, and law seemed boring, so he was sent to college in Paris to study religion. This was typical for a boy who was middle-class and intelligent, even one who did not seriously intend to become a priest.

ON TO PARIS

Like many boys who grow up in small towns, Diderot had dreams of the big city. Diderot did not know what profession he would pursue, but he imagined moving to Paris was a good start. Langres, Diderot's hometown, had a population of 10,000 or so. Paris, 200 miles (322 km) away, had more than half a million. The trip from Langres to Paris, which takes a few hours by car today, took seven days by horse-drawn carriage. When he arrived in Paris in 1728, he must have thought that he was in another world. Paris was a bustling and creative city where a young man could become, if not rich, famous.

When he graduated from the University of Paris a few years later, at the age of nineteen, Diderot had a rude awakening. His schooling was over, and it

The University of Paris, also known as the Sorbonne, was founded in 1150. In Diderot's time, and still today, the university was one of the most prestigious in Europe. Pictured above is the church of the Sorbonne, which is one of the most recognizable symbols of the university. Diderot graduated from the university in 1732.

was time for him to find a job. His father knew a lawyer from Langres who worked in Paris, and he suggested that Diderot study law with him. The lawyer agreed and took the young man in. A few months later, Diderot's father wrote to ask about his son's progress. He was disappointed to learn that Diderot wasn't doing so well—he didn't seem cut out for law after all. Frustrated and angry, Diderot's father wrote again. He instructed the lawyer to ask Diderot what profession he would prefer. According to biographer P. N. Furbank, Diderot responded, "None. I enjoy studying. I am well provided for and extremely content with life. I ask for nothing more."

When the slow mail carriage finally brought Diderot's response, his father was outraged. Did Diderot think his father had so much money that he could support a good-for-nothing son in the expensive city of Paris? He cut off Diderot's allowance and ordered him to come home at once.

Diderot ignored his father. Without money, a job, or a place to live, he was suddenly on his own in the big city. He did, at least, have an education. Since he was good at math, he began to support himself by tutoring children from wealthy families in the subject. Although tutoring did not pay very well, it gave Diderot a fair amount of freedom. He could work for an hour or two here, an hour or two there, and still find time to read, write, and explore the city.

Freedom was important to him. Once, he got a job as a tutor at the home of a wealthy businessman who paid him very well. However, he expected that Diderot would spend the whole day instead of an hour or two teaching the children. Diderot eventually gave up. A regular job was not for him.

MAKING ENDS MEET

During those early years in Paris, Diderot always chose adventure and freedom over security and comfort. Rather than selecting a career and sticking to it, he worked a variety of odd jobs. As a tutor, he moved from house to house. He also made money by doing a little writing. Since he was trained as a priest, he could write sermons, which paid fairly well. For the most part, however, he was extremely poor.

Paris is seen from a distance in this eighteenth-century engraving. Paris became Diderot's home after he moved there to attend the University of Paris. During Diderot's time, Paris served as the artistic and cultural capital of France and all of Europe. Today, the artistic legacy of the city has been preserved at the world-famous Louvre Museum and at numerous other museums and libraries throughout the city.

Diderot's situation was not unusual. Paris was full of educated young men trying to make money with their wits but barely getting enough to eat. Some of them were even worse off than Diderot. Once, when Diderot went to visit a writer friend, he was shocked at the man's living conditions. In the following excerpt from the book *Diderot and the Encyclopedists*, Diderot describes what he saw.

> I found him in a hole about as big as my fist, almost pitch-dark, without the smallest scrap of curtain or hanging to cover the nakedness

of his walls, a couple of straw-bottomed chairs, a truckle-bed with a quilt riddled by the moths, a box in the corner of the chimney and rags of every sort stuck upon it, a small tin lamp to which a bottle served as support, and on a shelf some dozen first-rate books.

Luckily for Diderot, a few people took pity on him and helped him out. Although Diderot's father had sworn not to give Diderot another dime, his mother sent him money in secret. His mother's maid, who delivered the money to him in Paris, contributed a little out of her own pocket. Once, when Diderot was sick with hunger, his landlady gave him a little toast and some wine. Her generosity taught Diderot a lesson. He swore that if he was able to help out, he would never refuse a person in need. And, in fact, when he was more successful later in life, he was generous with what he had.

INFLUENTIAL BOOKS

Diderot's early years in Paris were a time of unhappy struggle. Many years later, in his book *Rameau's Nephew*, he would remember this period as his "ten or twelve years of dragging through the mud in the streets of Paris." However, he was not just aimlessly drifting around Paris and not doing anything productive. In his spare time, he read as much as he could get his hands on.

One book in particular had a great impact on his thinking. It was a small book, hardly longer than the book you have in your hands right now, with the modest title *Philosophical Letters*. It contained twenty-five short essays about England and its religious beliefs, politics, literature, and science. The essays were written in the form of letters by a traveling Frenchman for his fellow countrymen back home.

At first glance, this book might not have seemed to be anything special. However, the title does suggest that there might be more to it. The word "philosopher" literally means "lover of knowledge." The title *Philosophical Letters* suggest that the author was not just someone on vacation, but rather someone with important ideas to share. These ideas would change Diderot's life forever. When he read *Philosophical Letters*, the struggling tutor decided once and for all what he would do with his life. He would become a philosopher, or as it is said in French, a *philosophe*.

VOLTAIRE AND ENGLISH PHILOSOPHY

CHAPTER 3

The author of *Philosophical Letters* was a wealthy Parisian named François Marie Arouet. As a young man, he had often been in trouble with the law for his vicious satires that were critical of society and its leadership. In 1716, for instance, Arouet had been banished from Paris on suspicion of writing a satirical poem about the regent, the Duke of Orléans. A year later he was sent to the Bastille, the notorious prison in Paris, after insulting a nobleman and challenging him to a duel. It was in prison that Arouet wrote some of the poems and plays that would eventually make him famous. Because of his circumstances, it was necessary for him to publish them under a pseudonym. He chose the name Voltaire.

Voltaire (1694–1778) is seen holding a copy of his book *The Henriade* in this portrait from 1736. *The Henriade* was a poem about Henry IV (1553–1610), one of the most beloved kings of France. Voltaire was an extremely versatile and prolific writer. Besides poetry, he also wrote plays, histories, philosophical works, and essays. Voltaire is best remembered for *Candide*, a novel about a young man who experiences a series of comic misadventures.

LADY MARY AND SIR ISAAC

In *Philosophical Letters*, Voltaire may have exaggerated the truth about England at times to make it seem freer and more equal than it really was. But he did not exaggerate the extraordinary accomplishments of English science. For instance, he reported on Lady Mary Wortley Montagu, who had discovered while traveling in the Middle East how to inoculate children for smallpox. This story alone must have caused quite a shock in France, a country in which it was not uncommon for kings to die of the disease. He also reported the great discoveries of Sir Isaac Newton, who had described the mathematical laws of the force of gravity. These were two of the greatest scientific discoveries of the eighteenth century, and Voltaire did much to popularize them in France.

Lady Mary Wortley Montagu (1689–1762) discovered how people in the Middle East protected themselves against smallpox. She brought knowledge of this procedure, known as inoculation, back to England.

Although Voltaire was let out of the Bastille after a year, he was arrested again in 1726 for fighting with an aristocrat and was banished to England. He wrote *Philosophical Letters* during this period of exile.

In *Philosophical Letters*, Voltaire describes aspects of English society, religion, government, science, literature, and philosophy that impressed him most. England, according to Voltaire, was a land of freedom and equality. In England, where literature and science flourished, religious differences were tolerated rather than punished, and even the peasants were middle class. In short, he suggested that England was the opposite of France in every way.

When *Philosophical Letters* was published in 1734, Voltaire was immediately recognized as one of the greatest minds of his age—and also one of the most controversial. He presented complex ideas in simple language that anyone could understand and wrote about serious topics with a sense of humor. These traits made Voltaire a role model for a whole generation of French writers, including Diderot.

Voltaire's influence on Diderot was particularly profound. Later in life, Diderot would address him as *mon cher maître* (my dear master). Above all, Diderot seems to have been impressed by Voltaire's account of the English philosophers Sir Francis

Bacon and John Locke. After reading *Philosophical Letters*, Diderot began to study the philosophy of these two men with great interest.

THE INFLUENCE OF BACON AND LOCKE

Francis Bacon was the founder of the modern scientific method. In his book *The Advancement of Learning* (1605), Bacon discussed the progress that science had made and suggested ways it could

Pictured above is the title page from a book by Francis Bacon (1561–1626) entitled *Essays; Religious Meditations, Places of Persuasion and Dissuasion*, published in 1597. The book was a collection of philosophical essays. In 1603, Bacon was knighted by the king of England and thus is commonly known as Sir Francis Bacon.

progress even further. He began by organizing all the branches of learning in relation to one another. Once knowledge was organized in this way, he argued, research could be carried out more efficiently and with better results.

John Locke was trained as a doctor. To discover the truth, he argued, it is not enough to sit around

John Locke (1632–1704) was an influential English philosopher. Besides inspiring Diderot, his ideas would also inspire the leaders of the American Revolution and the writers of the U.S. Constitution. Locke was one of the pioneers of the idea of human rights, or what are sometimes known as natural rights. These are the rights that belong to all people and include such things as life, liberty, and property.

thinking and studying books. Real knowledge, according to Locke, comes from people's experiences in the world around them. In his *Essay Concerning Human Understanding* (1690), Locke rejected the idea that human beings are born with any preexisting beliefs, or, as he called them, "innate ideas." Everything we know and believe, Locke argued, comes from experience. "From experience," he wrote, " . . . all our knowledge is founded, and from that it ultimately derives itself." His theory that all knowledge comes from the senses and people's experiences is called empiricism.

DIDEROT BECOMES A TRANSLATOR

To be able to read some of the new and exciting books that were being published in England, Diderot taught himself English. This skill would soon lead him to a job as a translator. There was a great demand in France for translations from English. Translating was not only easier than writing an original book, it also paid quite well. One of Diderot's first jobs as a translator, a long book on Greek history, paid well enough that he could live comfortably for a year.

By working as a translator, Diderot was finally able to lift himself out of the mud. *A History of*

Greece, which was finally published in 1743, was a success and immediately led to more work for Diderot. His next job was more difficult. It was a gigantic medical dictionary in three volumes, each of which weighed more than 10 pounds (4.5 kg). Even its title was long—*Medicinal Dictionary; Including Physic, Surgery, Anatomy, Chymistry, and Botany, in All Their Branches Relative to Medicine. Together with a History of Drugs; and an Introductory Preface, Tracing the Progress of Physic, and Explaining the Theories Which Have Principally Prevail'd in All Ages of the World.* Teaming with two other men to translate this dictionary, Diderot worked three full years.

Translation may seem like tedious work—mere copying from one language to another—and translating a dictionary may seem particularly tedious. But, for Diderot, translating the *Medicinal Dictionary* provided more than just work. As he translated, he learned about medicine, a subject that he had been curious about for some time. But medicine was not the only thing that Diderot learned translating the gigantic work. He also learned about science, about how important it was to get the big picture as well as the details, and how to collect facts side by side and arrange them in a logical order. He began to imagine how useful it might be to have an even bigger "dictionary," one that included not only medicine but all the sciences together. This dream would eventually lead to the *Encyclopedia*.

During these years, Diderot also began to take steps toward writing an original work of his own. In 1745, he published a translation of a small book by an English philosopher named Anthony Ashley Cooper, the Earl of Shaftesbury. In the book Diderot included some of his own notes and commentary. The earl had been tutored by John Locke and shared many of his beliefs. In the book that Diderot translated, *Inquiry Concerning Virtue and Merit*, Shaftesbury applied some of Locke's ideas to morals and ethics. Diderot's notes to this book are some of his first independent philosophical writing.

DIDEROT AND FRIENDS

CHAPTER 4

Working as a translator provided Diderot with more personal freedom than working as a tutor. It paid better as well. He had more time during the day to explore Paris and more money to spend enjoying himself. One of the first things he did with his newfound freedom was to fall in love.

Anne-Toinette Champion was three years older than Diderot. She came from a very poor family, but according to Diderot was as beautiful as an angel. Her mother was a widow, and the two women earned an honest living selling fabric. When Diderot and Champion first met, in 1741, Champion's mother was wary. After all, Diderot still had no regular job. Once Champion's mother found out what Diderot was paid for his translation of *A History of Greece*, however, she changed her mind. Perhaps he would make something of himself after all. She gave her permission for him to marry her daughter.

Diderot's parents, however, did not approve. Beautiful or not, Champion was poor, and Diderot's father would not allow his son to marry beneath him. When Diderot seemed ready to disobey and marry her anyway, his father called the police and had Diderot locked up in a monastery. That did not last long. Diderot crawled out a window and snuck back to Paris. He married Champion on November 6, 1743. He kept the marriage secret from his family.

DIDEROT MEETS ROUSSEAU

During his first year as a translator, Diderot met some of the intellectual companions who would shape his thought for the rest of his life. One day in 1742, when Diderot was passing time in a café, he was introduced to Jean-Jacques Rousseau, a young man who had just arrived in Paris. Rousseau was from Geneva, in what is now Switzerland. Rousseau had come to Paris with a scheme to get rich. He had developed a complicated mathematical system that he believed could be used for musical notation. He planned to sell it to some of the great musicians in Paris. However, the scheme came to nothing, and Rousseau resorted to working as a secretary in a

LES
CONFESSIONS
DE
J. J. ROUSSEAU,
Suivies

ᴧ

DES RÉVERIES
Du Promeneur Solitaire.

TOME PREMIER.

A GENEVE.

M. DCC. LXXXII.

Pictured above is the title page of *Les Confessions* (The Confessions) by Jean-Jacques Rousseau (1712–1778). This edition of the book was published in 1782. In *The Confessions*, Rousseau details the events of his fascinating life, including a tragic childhood in which his mother died and his father abandoned him. These events led to Rousseau fleeing his hometown of Geneva at the age of sixteen and traveling throughout Europe. In 1742, he arrived in Paris, where he would establish himself as an influential writer and philosopher.

wealthy family, just as Diderot had worked as a tutor to support himself.

Diderot and Rousseau had many other things in common. Rousseau, it turned out, was just a few months older than Diderot. Like Diderot, he loved music and mathematics. Both also liked to play chess. The two seemed destined to be friends. In some ways, though, Diderot and Rousseau were too similar. Their close friendship had a competitive side. Even twenty-five years later, Diderot still harbored a grudge about those chess games. In an essay from 1767, he recalls that Rousseau, who was by far the better player, would never agree to give him a handicap. The two friends would be competitive throughout their lives.

CONDILLAC AND D'ALEMBERT

Rousseau introduced Diderot to Etienne Bonnot de Condillac, a wealthy nobleman from the French town of Lyon. Condillac was born with such poor eyesight that he did not learn to read until he was twelve. Perhaps it was his own difficulties that made him interested in psychology, particularly how the five senses affect the way we learn. Like Diderot, Condillac was also probably influenced by Voltaire's *Philosophical Letters*. In imitation of John Locke's

Essay Concerning Human Understanding, Condillac had written a book called the *Essay on the Origin of Human Knowledge.* This book mixed some of the latest theories from England with some of Condillac's own ideas about how people learn. Condillac and Diderot had much to discuss.

It was not long before Diderot brought a fourth friend into the group of philosophers, Jean le Rond d'Alembert. D'Alembert was a bit younger than Diderot and Rousseau, but had already made a name for himself as a mathematician. D'Alembert had an unusual childhood. His mother was a wealthy aristocratic woman, while his father was a lieutenant general in the army. They were not married and did not want the scandal of an illegitimate child. The baby was abandoned on the steps of a church called Saint-Jean-le-Rond, which is where d'Alembert got his first name, Jean le Rond. Secretly, his father left quite a bit of money for him with the priest at the church. This money supported the boy later in life. Although he was adopted and raised by a family that was not wealthy, he was able to afford a good education and—unlike Diderot and Rousseau—never had to struggle to find work. When he got to Paris, he did not have to work as a tutor, but spent his time reading mathematics and attending lectures at the university.

In addition to being an editor of the *Encyclopedia*, Jean le Rond d'Alembert (1717–1783) was also a gifted mathematician and scientist. His talent is evidenced by the fact that Empress Catherine II of Russia tried to hire him as a tutor for her son. However, d'Alembert declined her offer. In Paris, d'Alembert was a frequent and honored guest at many of the best salons. In 1772, he was rewarded for his contributions to science and learning when he was named secretary of the prestigious French Academy.

The four friends—Diderot, Rousseau, Condillac, and d'Alembert—shared ideas and supported each others' work. They inspired each other to achieve what they otherwise might not have had the courage or the imagination to try. D'Alembert and Diderot likely discussed mathematics together. Rousseau gave Diderot the idea for a new kind of musical instrument—a mechanical organ with a built-in metronome to keep the beat. Diderot used his connections in the publishing industry to help Condillac find a publisher for his manuscript. Another idea they had was to publish a magazine, in which they could publish their own philosophical ideas. This idea never came to much, but it shows the cooperative spirit of this little circle.

THE *CYCLOPEDIA*

In 1746, Diderot was hired to do another translation comparable in size to the *Medicinal Dictionary. Cyclopedia, or Universal Dictionary of the Arts and Sciences*, by Ephraim Chambers, was originally published in English in 1728. By today's standards, it was somewhat longer and more detailed than an average dictionary, but not so detailed as a real encyclopedia—it was somewhere in between. An earlier attempt to translate Chambers's *Cyclopedia* had

A group of philosophers gathers for a meal and conversation in this engraving from the eighteenth century. The older gentleman with his hand up in the air is Voltaire, while Diderot is seated to his right.

failed when it turned out that the Englishman hired to do it really couldn't speak French well at all. Diderot, who already had a few good translations to his credit, was hired to fix the poor translation.

It was really too much work for one man alone, so Diderot brought on his friend d'Alembert to help him. Their job was not only to translate Chambers's book from English, but also to expand it a bit, too. Instead of two volumes, like the English edition, the French version would be five.

Translating Chambers's *Cyclopedia* was a bigger job than translating the *Medicinal Dictionary*.

Diderot and d'Alembert were not intimidated. In fact, Diderot suggested to his publisher that perhaps five volumes was not quite enough—perhaps eight would be better. Also, why not tack on two volumes of illustrations for good measure, making ten altogether? Suddenly the five-volume translation had doubled in size.

Gradually, as Diderot and d'Alembert planned a larger and larger expansion of Chambers's original two volumes, that reference work grew into something more recognizable as an encyclopedia, and became more and more of an original work rather than a translation. As far as the publishers were concerned, the longer the better—the more volumes they printed, the more money they could make. Also, there were rumors that other publishers were coming out with encyclopedias of their own, and surely the longest one would sell the best. Encouraged by their publishers and driven by their own ambition, Diderot and d'Alembert gradually transformed the translation of Chambers's *Cyclopedia* into the *Encyclopedia*.

DIDEROT'S FIRST ORIGINAL BOOK

However, it is one thing to plan an encyclopedia and another thing to write one. In 1746, Diderot had no

This writing set belonged to Diderot and can be found today at the Musée du Breuil in Langres, France. In Diderot's time, quill pens such as the one pictured were the most common writing instrument. A quill pen is made from the feather of a large bird, usually a goose. The hollow shaft of the feather, known as the quill, is cut to allow ink to rise into the shaft when dipped in an inkwell.

idea how difficult and important a job the *Encyclopedia* would become. He continued to work on other little projects, which are not so important in themselves but provide some insight into his thinking during this significant period of his life. That same year, for instance, Diderot published his first original book, *Pensées Philosophiques*, or *Philosophical Thoughts*. This little book was written in the form of aphorisms—brief, disconnected sentences and paragraphs—rather than one connected text. It contained many of Diderot's thoughts on religion and truth. "What is God?" he asks in one, then adds it is "a question which is asked of children, and which philosophers have a great deal of trouble in answering."

By this, Diderot did not mean to suggest that God does not exist. "I was born in the Roman Catholic church," he wrote in *Philosophical Thoughts*, "and I submit myself with all my strength to its decisions." What Diderot was really asking was how one knows anything about God. Where do one's ideas about God come from? What would John Locke's philosophy of empiricism tell us about God? If everything we know comes to us from our senses, how do we know anything about God? If we do know something about God, however, then perhaps it is empiricism that is wrong—perhaps not every idea comes to us from what we see and hear after all. These were not easy or obvious questions for Diderot. He was not sure he could find the answers to them. But, as a philosopher, he thought that it was important to think about them seriously and not just blindly accept other people's opinions on the matter. "What has never been put in question," he wrote, "has not been proved."

Although Diderot did not directly deny the teachings of the church, he knew that his book would be considered rebellious. He published his *Philosophical Thoughts* anonymously. Even though it was illegal to buy or sell, since it hadn't been approved by the censors, the book seems to have been popular. In fact, historians today suggest that many books became popular precisely because they were published secretly or banned. Even though he published his book anonymously, there were rumors circulating that Diderot was the author. He was on his way to making a name for himself as a philosopher.

THE POLICE CHASE DIDEROT

Meanwhile, the police had begun to notice Diderot. They had a network of informants who told them some of the rumors they were hearing about Diderot. One of the rumors that circulated was that Diderot was an atheist, which the police saw as a threat to public morals. Although they did not have enough evidence to arrest him yet, the police were keeping a careful watch and taking notes. They soon found out about his secret marriage, which they took as a sign that he was immoral. In many cases, they knew what Diderot was writing before he even tried to publish it. Nonetheless, they could not arrest him without hard evidence, such as a handwritten copy of *Philosophical Thoughts*. They searched his house once or twice, but found nothing.

1749

CHAPTER 5

The book that finally got Diderot in trouble was called *Letter on the Blind, for the Benefit of Those Who See*. Diderot wrote this book in 1749, in response to a real event.

That year, a famous surgeon in Paris announced that he was going to remove cataracts from a girl who had been born blind. The surgery was to restore her vision. This had never been done successfully in the past. All of Paris was excited to see what would happen.

Diderot and his friends were particularly curious about the experiment. If all our ideas came to us from our senses, as John Locke's philosophy of empiricism suggested, then perhaps the ideas of a blind person would be very different from our own. Obviously, she would have no idea what a color was—but would she be able to recognize objects by sight that she had once only been able to identify by touch? For example, when she regained her sight and looked at an apple, would she know what it was without touching it? All of the young philosophers wanted to watch her reaction at the moment she regained her sight.

THE QUESTION OF GOD

Unfortunately, the surgeon refused to let them watch the surgery itself, perhaps because he was frightened it would fail. Nonetheless, Diderot sat down to record his thoughts on the case. He compared it to a case he had heard about in England. In this instance, mathematician Nicholas Saunderson had become blind shortly after birth. Diderot had heard that Saunderson had developed a kind of abacus for doing math problems by hand. Saunderson, according to Diderot, was in a way the perfect empiricist. On his deathbed, according to Diderot in *Letter on the Blind*, Saunderson had said to the priest, "If you want me to believe in God, you must make me touch him."

By putting these words in Saunderson's mouth rather than his own, Diderot avoided saying outright that he didn't believe in God. Still, the questioning tone of *Letter on the Blind* was more daring than the

Nicholas Saunderson (1682–1739) lost his eyesight after contracting smallpox when he was one year old. However, his blindness did not prevent him from becoming one of England's finest mathematicians. Saunderson was a professor at the University of Cambridge and friends with many of the great minds of the day, including Sir Isaac Newton. In this portrait from 1719, Saunderson holds an armillary sphere, which was used to determine the location of stars and planets.

Diderot and his friends often gathered at a famous café named the Procope, seen in this engraving from the eighteenth century. The Procope opened in 1686 and was the first coffeehouse in Paris. The medallions that encircle the engraving are portraits of famous intellectuals who visited the café. Diderot is pictured in the center medallion on the left side.

earlier *Philosophical Thoughts*. It made many of its readers uncomfortable. Even Diderot's hero Voltaire, whom Diderot proudly sent a copy of *Letter on the Blind* as soon as it was published, was a bit shocked by the author's suggestions. He wrote Diderot a letter complimenting him on his excellent book, but asking for him to explain his religious beliefs.

Diderot was excited to receive a real letter from his role model, the author of the *Philosophical Letters*. He did not go so far as to deny the existence of God, Diderot explained to Voltaire in his reply, but he showed tolerance toward those who had different religious beliefs than his own, or even no religious beliefs at all. Diderot's religious beliefs could have been summarized as "to each their own."

Voltaire was impressed, but this wouldn't stop the church and police from pursuing Diderot. As far as the authorities were concerned, Diderot had gone too far. Diderot published his *Letter on the Blind* on June 3, 1749. Although he had not been so foolish to put his name on the book itself, he had spoken quite freely about it in the literary circles of Paris. It was not difficult for the police to identify him as the author. There were plenty of other writers in Paris who might have been jealous of Diderot, or who might have just been hungry enough to betray him for a small fee.

DIDEROT'S ARREST

At 7:30 in the morning on July 24, two policeman arrived at his door. Diderot had no choice but to let them in. They searched his apartment, but all they found were two printed copies of *Letter on the Blind*—not the handwritten manuscript that they needed to prove that Diderot was the author. Nonetheless, they arrested Diderot and brought him in for questioning.

Pictured above is a number of volumes of the first edition of the *Encyclopedia*. The complete *Encyclopedia* consisted of twenty-eight volumes. Within those volumes, there were more than 70,000 articles and about 3,000 illustrations. According to Diderot, the purpose of the *Encyclopedia* was to spread knowledge around the globe. As an editor, he was concerned about making sure all the information he provided was as up-to-date and accurate as possible. Although this was a difficult task, and numerous errors slipped by him, the volumes were still some of the most thoroughly researched books of their time.

This time, Diderot was not given the luxury of a monastery. He was locked in a tower in a grim castle at Vincennes, 6 miles (10 km) east of Paris. Under interrogation, he denied that he was the anonymous author of *Letter on the Blind* and *Philosophical Thoughts*. However, the police also questioned his publishers, who told a different story. Knowing the truth, the police decided to hold Diderot in the tower until he confessed.

Diderot gave up after three weeks. He signed a confession in August. That did not mean that he was free. He had still committed a crime, as far as the French government was concerned, and had to be punished. But, as a small reward, his jailers agreed to let him out of the tiny room he had been locked in, so long as he didn't leave the grounds of the castle itself. His wife and others were allowed to visit him and walk freely with Diderot in the gardens of the castle. Diderot was permitted to have some books and to keep working on the *Encyclopedia*. If he disobeyed in the least, however, or made any attempt to escape, all these little freedoms would be lost and he would be locked in the tower again.

RELEASE FROM PRISON

Although he was allowed to work on the *Encyclopedia* while in prison, it was very difficult to work efficiently. Diderot's publishers complained that the work they had paid him to do would not be done at this rate. D'Alembert also complained, since while Diderot was in prison, all the work became his responsibility. Finally the police agreed to let him go. Diderot was released from prison and returned to Paris on November 3, 1749.

"DISCOURSE ON THE ARTS AND SCIENCES"

Diderot's old friend Jean-Jacques Rousseau often walked the 6 miles (10 km) from Paris to visit Diderot in prison. Six miles on foot is a long way, and it was unusually hot that fall. Rousseau would usually stop along the way to rest in the shade and read a book or newspaper. On one of these breaks from his long walk, Rousseau read an announcement in the newspaper of a contest. Whoever wrote the best essay on the following question would win a prize: "Has progress

Jean-Jacques Rousseau, seen with a walking stick in this engraving, published his award-winning essay "Discourse on the Arts and Sciences" as a book in 1750. The themes discussed in this book would reappear in many of his later books including Discourse on the Origin of Equality *(1755) and* The Social Contract *(1762).*

in art and science improved the morals of mankind, or corrupted them?"

The question hit home with Rousseau. He wondered whether the civilized society of Paris was really more moral than primitive man had been—or whether the more society appeared to advance in some ways, the less admirable people really became. He thought about the question the rest of the way to the prison at Vincennes. When he finally reached the prison, he asked Diderot which side he should take. Diderot knew his friend well. According to historian Arthur M Wilson, he replied, "The side you'll take is the one no one else will." Rousseau agreed. He would argue that progress in the arts and sciences tended to corrupt our morals rather than improve them. This essay was called "Discourse on the Arts and Sciences." It won the prize a year later, and, with Diderot's help, it was published. It was immediately considered a masterpiece.

News of Diderot's arrest had spread quickly through Parisian society. The attempt to quiet him backfired, drawing attention to his work rather than silencing him. Wealthy German aristocrat Baron d'Holbach, who lived in Paris, invited Diderot and friends to his salon. Twice a week, at the baron's

Latourt pinx.

Robinson sculp. London

BARON D'HOLBACH

Paul-Henri Thiry, Baron d'Holbach (1723–1789), contributed many articles to the *Encyclopedia*, both as a writer and a translator. Beyond his work as a encyclopedist, d'Holbach was also an influential writer of philosophy. His best-known book was entitled *The System of Nature*. In this book, he questioned the existence of God. Because of this, the Catholic Church found the book offensive and demanded that it be forbidden. Other philosophers spoke out against the book, including Voltaire.

glamorous house, the encyclopedists met with the baron's aristocratic friends and discussed their radical ideas. Diderot invited the baron himself to write a few articles for the *Encyclopedia*. Eventually, the baron wrote more than a few, becoming one of the most important contributors.

Baron d'Holbach was particularly helpful to the editors of the *Encyclopedia* because he spoke German in addition to French and could serve as a translator. His skills were needed since a few large, scholarly works on the history of philosophy had been written in German. In science and technology, as well, there were a few important books that were only available in German—particularly books on mining and metalwork, two industries in which the Germans were the best in the world.

Baron d'Holbach's contributions to the *Encyclopedia* were significant. More important, however, was his work as a friend and a host. In a time without e-mail or television, and with very little advertising of any kind, the salon was an important way to spread information by word-of-mouth. There were salons almost every night of the week, each time at another house with different guests, often visiting from all over Europe. Rumors spread quickly in this chatty group. D'Holbach's salon helped spread the word about the *Encyclopedia* and attract contributors and subscribers long before the first volume was printed.

THE ANNOUNCEMENT OF THE *ENCYCLOPEDIA*

Finally, in November 1750, it was time to announce the publication of the first volume. Diderot wrote a prospectus, or announcement, which was printed up and sent out. The prospectus of 1750 is the first detailed description we have of the actual contents of the *Encyclopedia.*

The *Encyclopedia*, Diderot explained, would cover all of the sciences, all art and literature, and all of what he called "the mechanical arts," that is, craft and industry. In each area, experts would be hired. A priest would collect the articles on religion, while a lawyer would collect the articles on law, and so on. The prospectus explained Diderot's strategy.

> Thus each one, since he was concerned exclusively with a subject he understood, has been in a position to evaluate soundly what the ancients and moderns have written concerning it and to add knowledge drawn from his own supply to the resources they provided him. No one has

ENCYCLOPEDIE,

OU

DICTIONNAIRE RAISONNE

DES SCIENCES,

DES ARTS ET DES MÉTIERS,

PAR UNE SOCIETÉ DE GENS DE LETTRES.

Mis en ordre & publié par M. *DIDEROT*, de l'Académie Royale des Sciences & des Belles-Lettres de Pruſſe ; & quant à la PARTIE MATHEMATIQUE, par M. *D'ALEMBERT*, de l'Académie Royale des Sciences de Paris, de celle de Pruſſe, & de la Société Royale de Londres.

Tantùm ſeries junɛturaque pollet,
Tantùm de medio ſumptis accedit honoris! HORAT.

TOME PREMIER.

A PARIS,

Chez
{
BRIASSON, *rue Saint Jacques, à la Science.*
DAVID l'aîné, *rue Saint Jacques, à la Plume d'or.*
LE BRETON, Imprimeur ordinaire du Roy, *rue de la Harpe.*
DURAND, *rue Saint Jacques, à Saint Landry, & au Griffon.*
}

M. DCC. LI.

AVEC APPROBATION ET PRIVILEGE DU ROY.

This is the title page of Diderot and d'Alembert's *Encyclopedia* published in Paris in 1751. The title in French was *Encyclopédie, ou Dictionnaire Raisonne des Sciences, des Arts et des Metiers,* which translates into English as *Encyclopedia, or Reasoned Dictionary of the Sciences, Arts, and Crafts.* The illustration features an angel who radiates light. This can be seen as a metaphor in which the angel symbolizes the *Encyclopedia* and the light symbolizes wisdom, or knowledge, which is being provided by the *Encyclopedia.*

invaded the area of someone else or become involved with a subject that he may never have learned.

This division of labor made it possible for the *Encyclopedia* to cover a wider range of subjects than anything else of its kind.

This range was particularly clear with respect to the mechanical arts. These articles, Diderot explained, would be the most original and the most difficult. Information on art and science could be found in books, but it was far more difficult to find accurate information on how to make socks or bricks. The son of a cutler, Diderot knew that the secrets of the artisans had never been written down but were passed from father to son and from master to apprentice. According to his prospectus, the fundamental flaw that Diderot saw in Chambers's *Cyclopedia*—the book he had been hired to translate—was that "Chambers read books, but he saw scarcely any artisans; however there are many things that one learns only in the workshops." Later in the prospectus, Diderot explained how he and d'Alembert went about solving this problem.

Everything impelled us to go directly to the workers. We approached the most capable of them in Paris and in the realm. We took the trouble of going into their shops, of questioning them, of writing at their dictation, of developing their thoughts and of drawing therefrom the terms particular to their professions, of setting up tables of these terms and of working out definitions for them . . . and of correcting through long and frequent conversations with others what some of them imperfectly, obscurely, and sometimes unreliably had explained.

By including this everyday, practical knowledge alongside articles on religion, philosophy, history, and law, Diderot and d'Alembert made it clear that their *Encyclopedia* was for everyone, not just the very educated. The prospectus stated, "Both the man of the people and the scientist will always have equally as much to desire and instruction to find in an encyclopedia." By putting the practical knowledge of the worker together with the less practical, more abstract knowledge of the philosopher, they expressed their belief in the inherent equality, worth, and intelligence of all different classes of people. This was a powerful and controversial statement to make in the pyramid-shaped society of the ancien régime.

Charles Panckoucke aux auteurs de l'Encyclopédie

In 1746, Diderot (*bottom*) was hired to translate from English into French a book called the *Cyclopedia*. Because of the complexity of the project, he recruited his friend Jean le Rond d'Alembert (*top*) to help him. Together, the two men transformed the translation of the *Cyclopedia* into the *Encyclopedia*. The two brought their own unique talents to the project. Diderot was especially good at recruiting contributors, while d'Alembert used his expertise to contribute to the organization of the *Encyclopedia* and edit the science and math articles.

Eight thousand copies of the prospectus were printed and sent out. Even before the first volume of the *Encyclopedia* was printed, the prospectus caused controversy. What the editors had promised did not seem possible. How could their book contain all the subjects that they promised it would contain? Moreover, as they themselves seemed to admit, much of the book would be just translated and plagiarized from sources like Chambers's *Cyclopedia*. The prospectus made some big promises. Would the *Encyclopedia* itself really be so original, or so accurate, as the authors claimed it would be? Would it ever even be finished?

THE ENCYCLOPEDIA

Any doubts and criticisms were answered by the first volume of the *Encyclopedia*, which was received by subscribers in July 1751. It was almost 1,000 pages long and contained articles on almost everything imaginable beginning with the letter A. The introduction alone, written by d'Alembert, was almost 100 pages. Whereas Diderot's prospectus had explained in a matter-of-fact way what the *Encyclopedia* would contain, d'Alembert's introduction—or, as he called it, "Preliminary Discourse"— laid out some of the more abstract philosophical principles behind the editing and arrangement of this massive work. This introduction is an important source of information about the ideas that went into the editing of the *Encyclopedia*.

The "Preliminary Discourse" is divided into three parts. In the first part, d'Alembert explains John Locke's theory of empiricism. "All our direct knowledge," d'Alembert writes, "can be reduced to what we receive through our senses; whence it follows that we owe all our ideas to our sensations." He also admits that he was influenced by Francis Bacon's ideas about the proper organization of science. Bacon had stressed that merely collecting facts was not enough. It was just as important to organize them and to understand the relationships between them. In this section, the influence of Diderot on d'Alembert is particularly clear. It is Diderot, under the influence of Voltaire, who first drew d'Alembert's attention to these two great English philosophers.

In the second part of his "Preliminary Discourse," d'Alembert discusses the history of the arts and sciences after the end of the Middle Ages. He names the contributions of Bacon, Locke, and Isaac Newton. In the third part, d'Alembert included an edited version of Diderot's original prospectus, which described in more detail the actual contents of the *Encyclopedia*. Lastly, d'Alembert included a chart showing how the various subjects covered in the *Encyclopedia* related to one another.

Diderot himself contributed articles to the first volume on subjects as varied as Arabs, Aristotle, and art. Articles like these were unlikely to cause controversy. More controversial, however, was his article on authority. "No man," he wrote, "has received from nature the right of commanding others." Needless to say, this was a controversial thing to say in a monarchy. Although he did not explicitly call for revolution, Diderot suggested quite openly that the power of the king ultimately depended on the will of his subjects to obey.

THE FIRST VOLUMES

According to Diderot's original prospectus, the *Encyclopedia* would be in eight volumes, with two volumes of plates (printed illustrations) at the end, for a total of ten volumes. After the first volume was

At right is an illustrated page from the *Encyclopedia*. The finished *Encyclopedia* consisted of eleven volumes of illustrations similar to the one pictured here. The title of this illustration is "Dessein, Mains," which in French means "anatomy of the hands." The illustration shows the various ways the hands can be shaped. The illustration is intended to show the sophistication of the structure of the hands and how they are specially designed to perform a wide variety of tasks and make many different gestures.

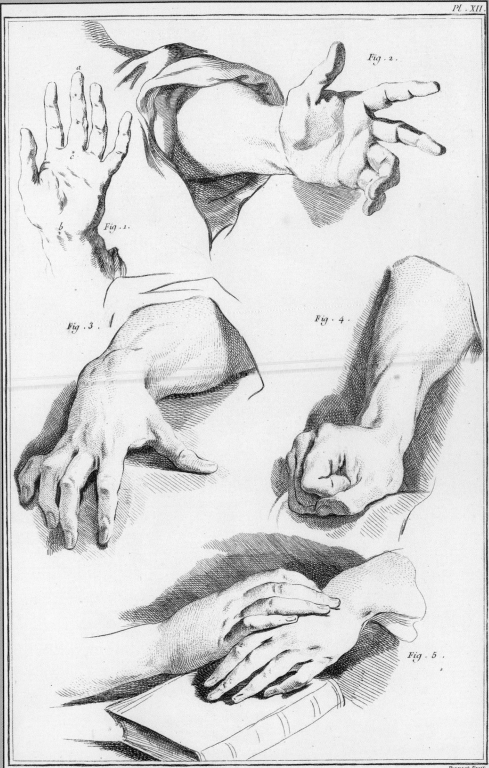

Pl. XII.

Fig. 2.

Fig. 1.

Fig. 3.

Fig. 4.

Fig. 5.

Prevost Fecit

Dessein, Mains.

published in 1751, one volume would come out every six months. At that rate, the entire *Encyclopedia* would be published by 1755 or so. That plan turned out to be overly optimistic. The second volume, covering B to some of C, came out on schedule in January 1752, but the third volume was not issued until October 1753—more than a year late. Volume IV was published a year after that, and volume V was not released until November 1755. That was the year that the *Encyclopedia* was supposed to be finished, according to the original plan. However, they had only completed A through E.

The *Encyclopedia* was clearly going to be much longer than they had planned, and it was going to take a longer time to publish. The publishers didn't mind, since the more volumes they published, the more money they made. Some of the contributors, however, began to get discouraged. They had imagined that they would work on the *Encyclopedia* for five years or so—but five years had gone by and they were only on the fifth letter of the alphabet.

Nonetheless, the fifth volume of the *Encyclopedia* was exciting. Voltaire wrote the articles on elegance, eloquence, and spirit (*esprit*). One of the publishers of the *Encyclopedia* wrote the article on copyright (*droit de copie*). Rousseau wrote on economy, an article in which he expressed for the first time some of the ideas that would eventually make him famous. Diderot himself wrote quite a few articles on topics as varied as natural right (*droit naturel*) and Egyptians, as well as more articles on industrial production, such as the distillation of brandy (*eau-de-vie*) and the manufacture of enamel. But many considered the most exciting article of all in the D–E volume of the *Encyclopedia* to be the article on the encyclopedia.

In the first paragraph of this article, Diderot expresses pride. He knows that his book will be a symbol of the time in which he lived. He expresses optimism about the future, and a faith that civilization will make progress.

> Encyclopedia, n. f. This word signifies *chain of knowledge*; it is composed of the Greek preposition *en* (in), and the nouns *kyklos* (circle) and *paideia* (knowledge). Indeed, the purpose of an *encyclopedia* is to collect knowledge disseminated around the globe; to set forth its general system to the men with whom we live, and transmit it to those who will come after us, so that the work of preceding centuries will not become useless to the centuries to come; and that our offspring, becoming better instructed, will at the same time become more virtuous and

happy, and that we should not die without having rendered a service to the human race.

At the same time that he is proud, however, Diderot is also humble. Having worked hard already for more than five years, Diderot understands that the job he and his friends have taken on just might be impossible. One similar group of editors, he notes, took sixty years just to write a dictionary— but a dictionary, he adds, is not as complex as an encyclopedia. As he worked on the *Encyclopedia*, Diderot discovered many difficulties, which he describes in his article on the encyclopedia.

A FEW SHORTCOMINGS

Among the difficulties Diderot faced included his initial plan to divide the labor among many experts. This approach led to many inconsistencies between

This illustration from the *Encyclopedia* shows how silkworms are cultivated in the French silk-making process. The top panel shows how workers grow and care for the silkworm and the equipment that they use. The bottom panel shows the phases in the life of a silkworm. This illustration is an example of a topic that Diderot wanted to make known to a wide range of people. Before the *Encyclopedia*, extensive knowledge of silk-making would have been limited to people who worked in the industry.

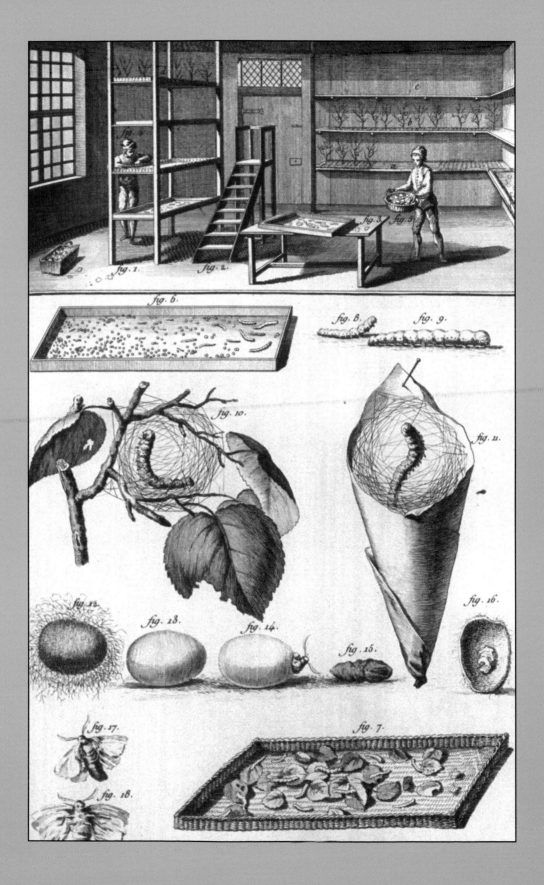

fig. 1. fig. 2.

fig. 6.

fig. 8. fig. 9.

fig. 10.

fig. 11.

fig. 12.

fig. 13. fig. 14.

fig. 15.

fig. 16.

fig. 17.

fig. 7.

fig. 18.

articles. The tone and style changed from article to article. Some articles were longer than necessary, while others were too short. Also, Diderot admitted, there was no way he himself could check every article. "In spite of all the care we have taken, there have been some gross blunders," he wrote in his article on the encyclopedia, as well as "whole articles that do not have a shadow of common sense."

Another interesting problem that Diderot mentions concerns another part of his original plan, which was to interview craftsmen and workers. What he discovered was that many of these artisans were not eager to share the secrets of their trade. They were suspicious of these strange men who came to their shops and asked them detailed questions. Were they police or tax collectors sent to find out how much money they were making? If the secrets of the trade, which had been passed on for generations from father to son, were collected together in one book that anyone could buy, what would stop others from opening competing businesses? This, Diderot wrote in his article, explained some of the errors in the *Encyclopedia*—many of his "informants" had simply lied.

Reading Diderot's article on the encyclopedia, we see how much things have changed in the five years since his optimistic prospectus. Writing an encyclopedia turned out to be much harder than he had expected.

Nonetheless, the problems that he had in the beginning were not so serious as the problems to come.

RESISTANCE TO THE *ENCYCLOPEDIA*

The sixth and seventh volumes of the *Encyclopedia* were published in 1756 and 1758. However, a series of events threatened the completion of the work. First, in January 1757, an assassin snuck into Versailles and attacked Louis XV with a small knife. The king was not seriously wounded, but many people thought that the crime was a symbol of more widespread disobedience. Without good reason, many people blamed the *Encyclopedia* for corrupting public morals.

Second, in 1758, philosopher Claude Adrien Helvétius published his book *On Spirit*, which, it seemed, was heavily influenced by the *Encyclopedia* but even more outrageous in tone. To some politicians, this book was further proof that the dangerous ideas of the *Encyclopedia* were spreading. Third, when the seventh volume of the *Encyclopedia* was issued, it started a controversy that almost doomed the whole project once and for all.

One article in particular, d'Alembert's essay on Geneva, was the main source of the controversy. It was Voltaire, that old troublemaker, who had encouraged d'Alembert to write it. Like Voltaire's letter on England, d'Alembert's article on Geneva was, on the surface, nothing but objective facts about a foreign place. However, d'Alembert slyly used this description to criticize French society. In particular, in his description of the religion in Geneva, d'Alembert seemed to suggest that the religious beliefs imposed by law in France were too strict, and that Geneva was a far more lenient society. In fact, although Geneva was not Catholic like France, it was not at all as free as d'Alembert suggested. The Genevan priests were offended by his suggestion that they did not carefully protect the morals and religious beliefs of their small state. D'Alembert managed to offend the priests in his own country as well, and was attacked on both sides.

For his part, Diderot did not quite openly criticize d'Alembert, but he did not support him either. Rousseau—who grew up in Geneva—took offense at what d'Alembert had written. He announced publicly that he would have nothing more to do with the *Encyclopedia*. D'Alembert, upset by all the criticism he had received and disappointed that Diderot had not defended him, also quit. After fifteen years, the circle of friends was dissolving.

THE KING BANS THE *ENCYCLOPEDIA*

The authorities, meanwhile, were cracking down. In another time, perhaps, they might have ignored d'Alembert's article. After all, it had been approved in advance by the censor. But after the attack on Louis XV, the climate was much less tolerant. After many years of being suspicious of the *Encyclopedia*, the authorities finally decided to bring an end to it. On March 8, 1759, by royal order of Louis XV himself, the *Encyclopedia* was banned. "The advantages to be derived from a work of this sort, in respect to progress in the arts and sciences," the king wrote, "can never compensate for the irreparable damage that results from it in regard to morality and religion."

After only seven volumes, which ended with the letter G, the *Encyclopedia* was officially illegal. The publishers were ordered to return the money that had been paid in advance for subscriptions. After more than a decade, it looked like the *Encyclopedia* would never be finished. Diderot's friend Rousseau had moved out of Paris, and his coeditor d'Alembert

Louis XV (1710–1774) was the great-grandson of King Louis XIV. He was born at the Palace of Versailles and became king when he was only five years old. However, the Duke of Orléans ran the government for him until he was fourteen years old. Early in his reign, Louis earned the nickname the Well-Beloved, but by the end of his reign he was generally disliked by the people of France and considered to be an ineffective ruler.

had also abandoned him. The *Encyclopedia*, it seemed, had brought nothing but trouble.

The official ban alone would not have prevented Diderot from working on the *Encyclopedia*. After all, he had published books illegally before. But by 1759, he was older and less adventurous than he had been as a young man. His colleagues had also left, which made the already difficult task of editing the *Encyclopedia* seem impossible. More than anything else, Diderot needed a break. According to historian Otis Fellows, Diderot wrote to his mentor Voltaire, "My dear master, I am well past the age of forty; I am tired of all the chicanery. From morning to evening I cry out for peace, only peace, and there is scarcely a day I am not tempted to go and live unnoticed and die serene in the province from whence I came."

THE FINAL YEARS

Since 1757, as the controversy surrounding the *Encyclopedia* heated up, Diderot had been spending time with one of the few friends he had left, the Baron d'Holbach, at the baron's estate outside of Paris. Here, he could get his mind off the *Encyclopedia* and work on other things. He wrote a few plays, which he published along with essays on art and theater. These writings show the broad range of Diderot's interests as well as his application of the ideals of Enlightenment outside of philosophy, politics, and religion.

In his plays, Diderot applied some of the same principles that he had used in writing the *Encyclopedia*. Just as the *Encyclopedia* had included everyday subjects, Diderot's plays portrayed the lives of working people, not just kings and queens. In his art criticism, similarly, he preferred the paintings of Jean-Baptiste Greuze, who portrayed the life of every-day French peasants, to the paintings of François Boucher, who portrayed the flowery life at the top of the pyramid of French society.

Writing plays and art criticism provided relief but not complete satisfaction for Diderot. From time to time he would pick up his pen and write an article or two for the *Encyclopedia*, even though he was not sure that it would ever be published. This work had to be done in secret. Diderot kept his door locked and any manuscripts out of sight. Working slowly but steadily, he gradually compiled article after article, volume after volume.

FINISHING THE TASK

Many of the articles in the last section of the *Encyclopedia* were written before the ban in 1759. After the ban, for obvious reasons, it was more difficult to get new contributors. Diderot wrote many of the articles himself. Because he didn't sign his name to them, we don't know the exact number—perhaps a few hundred. A few other brave souls continued to contribute even after the ban. Diderot's friend the Baron d'Holbach wrote more than 1,000 articles, all told. But the real champion of the latter

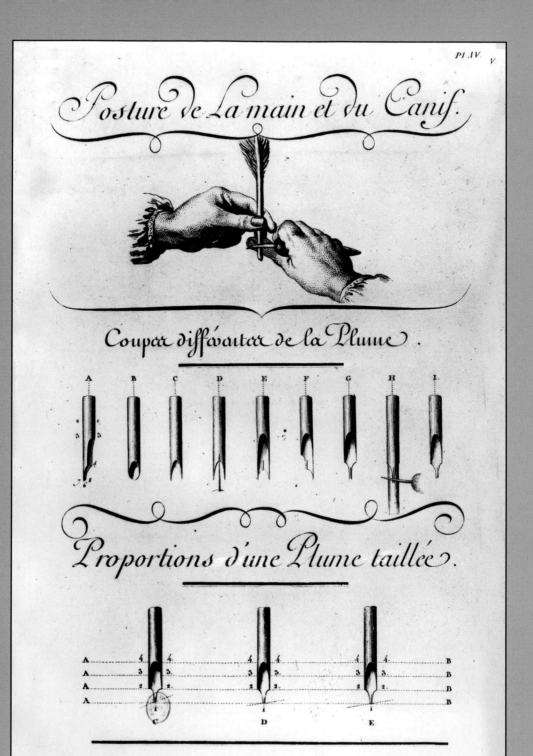

This illustration from the *Encyclopedia* depicts the manufacturing of quill pens. The top panel shows how an instrument called a penknife is held so that it can cut a point on the quill. The bottom two panels show the various quill cuts and their dimensions.

volumes of the encyclopedia was Louis de Jaucourt. Using four or five secretaries at once and working as much as fourteen hours a day, Jaucourt eventually contributed more than 17,000 individual entries, totalling almost 5 million words, to the seventeen volumes of the *Encyclopedia*.

Besides writing, there was the difficult task of reviewing what had been written, compiling the articles together, and organizing the illustrations. Diderot did this immense task on his own. The final ten volumes alone contained a total of 11 million words, or roughly 1,000 times as many as the book you are holding in your hands.

As if the size alone were not discouraging enough, there was also constant insecurity. Diderot, working behind locked doors, had no guarantee that the *Encyclopedia* would ever see the light of day. At any moment police inspectors could knock at the door and seize the manuscripts in his possession. If they caught him working on the banned work, Diderot would probably be thrown in jail for the last time.

During these long and lonely years, Diderot was having a hard time making ends meet. He was a father and a husband as well as an encyclopedist. Without a steady source of income from subscribers, his family had no income. This made it especially difficult for him to finish his work. After careful consideration, he decided to sell his library—the books that he had collected over the years as well as many of his own manuscripts.

A GIFT FROM CATHERINE THE GREAT

In 1765, in desperation, he wrote a letter offering his collection to Empress Catherine II of Russia (also known as Catherine the Great). Upon receiving her reply, Diderot was surprised to see that she not only would buy his library, but would hire him to maintain it for her as well. Diderot would be able to keep his books and receive an annual salary. Only when he died would his collection be sent to Russia. This generous offer allowed Diderot to continue working on the *Encyclopedia* free of distractions. With renewed energy—sometimes working as much as ten hours a day, seven days a

In 1773, Diderot traveled to St. Petersburg, Russia, to meet Empress Catherine II. Catherine assisted many artists and writers, including Diderot, so that they would help establish Russia as an important center for the arts and literature. Interestingly, Catherine was not Russian but German. Her real name was Sophie Friederike Auguste von Anhalt-Zerbst. She changed her name to Catherine after she married the grandson of Peter the Great, a legendary Russian ruler. Catherine became empress in 1762.

ON THE PHILOSOPHER

Of the thousands of articles in the final ten volumes, one deserves special mention. Although its author is unknown, it expresses in a few pages some of the basic ideals that guided the *Encyclopedia*. It is the article on the philosopher in volume twelve.

Whether or not this article was written by Diderot himself, it expresses Diderot's fundamental belief that the philosopher should not isolate himself with his books. Instead, the philosopher should live among the people, studying them, learning from them, and teaching them what he has learned.

Man is not a monster who must live only in the abyss of the sea or in the depths of a forest. The very necessities of life make communicating with others necessary to him. In whatever state he may find himself, his needs and well-being draw him to live in society. Thus reason compels him to know, to study, and to work to acquire sociable qualities. A philosopher does not find himself in exile in this world; he does not at all believe himself to be in enemy territory . . . he wishes to find pleasure with others, and in order to do so, he must give it . . . He is an honorable man who wishes to please and to make himself useful.

After twenty years of work on the *Encyclopedia*, the ideal of the philosopher continued to inspire Diderot, just as it had when he was young.

week—he set to work. Once he had finished putting the ten volumes of articles together, he began to assemble the illustrations, another eleven volumes. By the end of the year, the *Encyclopedia* was, after twenty years of hard work, finally ready for publication. To get past the king's ban of the *Encyclopedia*, Diderot waited until all the volumes were printed before sending them out. This allowed him to quickly deliver the entire *Encyclopedia* to his subscribers before the authorities could intervene.

When the final ten volumes of the *Encyclopedia* appeared, plus the eleven volumes of illustrations, in 1765, Diderot had accomplished his life's work. What had begun as a humble translation of a two-volume English dictionary had

Jean-Baptiste Greuze (1725–1805) drew this portrait of Diderot using black and white chalk on brown paper. Greuze was one of the most popular artists in France during his lifetime and his realistic style influenced many other French painters. The subjects of his paintings were often humble peasants depicted at work or in their homes. Diderot often wrote favorably of Greuze's paintings, believing that they were honest portrayals of everyday life.

grown to twenty-eight volumes in all—seventeen volumes of text and another eleven volumes of illustrations.

Diderot spent his last years in various ways. He wrote more art criticism and a few more minor books here and there. In part to express his gratitude to Catherine II for coming to his aid at a difficult time in his life, he wrote a plan for public education for her. This plan explained what and how the young people of Russia should learn at school. This was one of his last contributions to posterity. He died peacefully on July 31, 1784. As promised, his books and manuscripts were sent to Russia, where to this day they are treasured in the national library there.

THE DISCOVERY OF *RAMEAU'S NEPHEW*

That, however, is not the end of Diderot's story. Gradually, in the years after he died, various manuscripts of his were discovered. These were books that he had written but decided not to publish. Some had passed through his family, others had been entrusted to friends. Among these unpublished manuscripts was one discovered in 1804 in Germany. This manuscript was believed to be a German translation of an unpublished work by Diderot called *Rameau's Nephew*. But the original French manuscript was lost,

The French are immensely proud of the accomplishments of Diderot. In the city of Arles, there is even a street named after him. Seen above is a view down Rue Diderot, or Diderot Street.

and, without it, there was no way to tell whether this German version was actually a hoax. The mystery remained unsolved for eighty-five years. Finally, in 1890, in an old book of plays for sale by a bookseller in Paris, the original manuscript was discovered. The manuscript was determined to be in Diderot's own handwriting, thereby proving that he was, in fact, the author of *Rameau's Nephew*.

This strange book is something between a play, a novel, and a philosophical essay. It is written in dialogue form, but clearly intended to be read rather than watched on a stage.

Rameau's Nephew records an imaginary conversation between Diderot and a young man named Rameau, the nephew of a famous Parisian composer of the same name. Rameau, a young rascal struggling to make it in Paris, bears an interesting resemblance to Diderot himself as a young man. In fact, *Rameau's Nephew* may be read as a strange sort of autobiography, in which Diderot, now a famous philosopher, meets his younger self.

RAMEAU'S MIXED-UP MORALS

Rameau, Diderot tells us, is full of contradictions. "Today, in dirty linen and ragged breeches, tattered and almost barefoot, he slinks along with head down and you might be tempted to call him over and give him money. Tomorrow, powdered, well shod, hair curled, beautifully turned out, he walks with head high, showing himself off, and you would almost take him for a gentleman." His morals are as mixed-up as his physical appearance. He does not seem to know the difference between good and bad and seems not to care, either. Everywhere he goes, he causes trouble, contradicting people and starting arguments.

In many ways, Diderot tells us, Rameau is not likable or trustworthy. Nonetheless, Diderot finds people of his kind interesting "because their characters

contrast sharply with other people's and break the tedious uniformity that our social conventions and set politeness have brought about . . . He stirs people up and gives them a shaking, makes them take sides, brings out the truth, shows who are really good and unmasks the villains."

TWO SIDES OF RAMEAU

The two characters of *Rameau's Nephew* represent the two sides of the author's true self. The Diderot character represents the mature philosopher, who wants to arrange things in an orderly fashion and to figure them out. The Rameau character represents the mischievous child inside, who wants to unmask pretenders and challenge convention. Throughout his life, the editor of the *Encyclopedia* combined both of these aspects in one person.

The story that Diderot tells in *Rameau's Nephew* can also be interpreted as a story about his

Public monuments are often constructed to honor exceptional citizens and their contributions to the national culture. In France, Diderot is memorialized by this statue in Paris. The bronze statue is located on the Boulevard Saint-Germain, one of the most famous and fashionable streets in the city. The statue was created by French sculptor Jean Gautherin in the nineteenth century.

masterpiece, the *Encyclopedia*. After all, that book also had two sides to it. On the one hand, it did what all works of reference do—it collected the facts together in order in a way that was, on the face of it, easy to understand. On the other hand, the *Encyclopedia* stirred things up, causing a bit of trouble and challenging people's assumptions.

DIDEROT'S LEGACY

As we have seen, from his school days, Diderot was both rebellious and smart. He had the courage to strive for goals that seemed dangerous or impossible, as well as the patience to keep working when other people lost hope. The *Encyclopedia* proved that the human mind is capable of great things. Although many great books were written during the Enlightenment, books that would change the world, none symbolized the period quite like the *Encyclopedia*. Created by many people working together, it captured the spirit of its time and place. But it would not have been possible without the courage, patience, and reason of one man: Denis Diderot.

TIMELINE

1713	Diderot is born in Langres, France.
1715	Louis XIV dies; Philippe II, Duke of Orléans, is appointed regent for Louis XV.
1728	Diderot moves from Langres to Paris.
1732	Diderot graduates from the University of Paris and begins work as a tutor.
1734	Voltaire's *Philosophical Letters* is published.
1743	Diderot secretly marries Anne-Toinette Champion.
1745	Diderot translates Shaftesbury's *Inquiry Concerning Virtue and Merit*.
1746	Diderot is hired to translate Ephraim Chambers's *Cyclopedia*.
1749	Diderot is arrested and put in prison at Vincennes.
1750	Diderot publishes the prospectus of the *Encyclopedia*.
1751	The first volume of the *Encyclopedia* is published.
1759	The *Encyclopedia* is banned after seven volumes.
1765	Diderot sells his library to Catherine the Great and finishes the *Encyclopedia*.
1784	Diderot dies in Paris.
1804	*Rameau's Nephew* is discovered in Germany.

Glossary

abacus An instrument used for math calculations by sliding beads along rods.

abstract An idea that is very general and that doesn't relate directly to things.

ancien régime The period in French history beginning in 1651 and ending with the French Revolution in 1789.

apprentice A beginner; a worker being trained by someone more skilled.

aristocrat A noble person, such as a duke or duchess, lord, baron, etc.

artisan A skilled craftsman.

atheist Someone who does not believe in God.

bourgeois A middle-class person, such as a businessman or shopkeeper.

cataract A clouding of the lens of the eye that affects the ability to see.

censors The government workers who control what is published.

chenille Fabric with a fuzzy texture.

chicanery Mischief or trickery.

corsage The waist area of a dress.

court The large, open part of the palace where nobles meet with the king or queen. Also, the name given to the nobles who make up the king or queen's inner circle of friends and advisers.

cutler An artisan who makes knives, scissors, and other cutting tools.

empiricism The theory that all knowledge comes from things we experience.

encyclopedist Someone who works on an encyclopedia.

estate One of the three groups under the king in the ancien régime: the church, the aristocracy, and the rest of the population.

handicap An advantage given to a weaker player to make a game more even.

illegitimate Born to parents who are not married.

inoculate To expose to a germ in order to develop immunity to the germ.

Jesuit A member of an organization within the Roman Catholic Church who is dedicated to teaching others about the church and its beliefs.

metronome A device that beats regularly to help musicians keep their rhythm.

Middle Ages A period of history from about AD 500–1500. Sometimes called the Dark Ages.

monarchy A country that is ruled by one person, such as a king or a queen.

natural right A right that is granted to each person by nature or God as opposed to a right that is granted by a government.

peasant A farmworker who owns little or no land.

philosophe French for "philosopher," this word was used in Diderot's time to mean someone who uses reason for the good of humanity.

philosophy A study of values and logic. In Greek, literally, the love of knowledge and truth.

posterity The future generations of people.

prospectus A proposal; a detailed announcement of something.

regent Someone who rules temporarily when the rightful heir to a throne is too young.

salon An informal gathering for the purpose of discussing art and ideas. The gathering place, such as a living room or an apartment, is also called a salon.

satire Literature that is humorous and critical of the behavior of an individual or a society.

tithe A small tax.

FOR MORE INFORMATION

American Society for Eighteenth-
  Century Studies
P.O. Box 7867
Wake Forest University
Winston-Salem, NC 27109
(336) 727-4694
Web site: http://asecs.press.jhu.edu

Canadian Society for Eighteenth-
  Century Studies
Department of English
University of Ottawa
Ottawa, Ontario, Canada K1N 6N5
Web site: http://www.c18.org/
  scedhs-csecs/index.html

Center for Seventeenth- and
  Eighteenth-Century Studies
310 Royce Hall
University of California at
  Los Angeles
Los Angeles, California 90095-1404
(310) 206-8552
Web site: http://www.humnet.ucla.edu/
  humnet/c1718cs/

Voltaire Foundation
University of Oxford
99 Banbury Road
OX2 6JX
UK
+44 (0)1865 284600
Web site: http://www.voltaire.ox.ac.uk

WEB SITES

Due to the changing nature of Internet links, the Rosen Publishing Group, Inc., has developed an online list of Web sites related to the subject of this book. This site is updated regularly. Please use this link to access the list:

http://www.rosenlinks.com/phen/dide

FOR FURTHER READING

Diderot, Denis. *Rameau's Nephew*. London, England: Penguin, 1966.

Dunn, John. *The Enlightenment*. San Diego, CA: Lucent, 1999.

Fellows, Otis. *Diderot*. Boston, MA: Twayne, 1989.

Gillispie, Charles, ed. *A Diderot Pictorial Encyclopedia of Trades and Industry*. New York, NY: Dover, 1993.

Goubert, Pierre. *The Ancien Régime*. New York, NY: Harper, 1974.

Goubert, Pierre. *The Course of French History*. New York, NY: Franklin Watts, 1998.

Kallen, Stuart, A. *The 1700s*. Farmington Hills, MI: Greenhaven, 2001.

BIBLIOGRAPHY

D'Alembert, Jean le Rond. *Preliminary Discourse to the Encyclopedia of Diderot*. Indianapolis, IN: Bobbs-Merrill, 1963.

Darnton, Robert. *The Great Cat Massacre*. New York, NY: Random House, 1985.

Diderot, Denis. *Rameau's Nephew*. London, England: Penguin, 1966.

Doyle, William, ed. *Old Regime France 1648–1788*. New York, NY: Oxford University Press, 2001.

Fellows, Otis. *Diderot*. Boston, MA: Twayne Publishers, 1989.

Funck-Brentano, Frantz. *The Old Regime in France*. New York, NY: Longmans, Green, 1929.

Furbank, P. N. *Diderot: A Critical Biography*. New York, NY: Knopf, 1992.

Gendzier, Stephen J., ed. and trans. *Denis Diderot's The Encyclopedia; Selections*. New York, NY: J. & J. Harper Editions, 1969.

Lough, John. *The Contributors to the Encyclopédie*. London, England: Grant and Cutler: 1973.

Lough, John. *The Encyclopédie.* London, England: Longmans, 1971.

Lough, John. *Essays on the Encyclopédie of Diderot and D'Alembert.* London, England: Oxford University Press, 1968.

Morley, John. *Diderot and the Encyclopedists.* London, England: Macmillan and Co., 1886.

Scholarly Publishing Office of the University of Michigan Library. "The Encyclopedia of Diderot and d'Alembert." Retrieved January 2005 (http://www.hti.umich.edu/d/did).

Wilson, Arthur M. *Diderot.* New York, NY: Oxford University Press, 1972.

INDEX

ABOUT THE AUTHOR

Sam Stark studied eighteenth-century philosophy at Columbia University. Like Diderot, he works as a translator and an editor.

CREDITS

Like **Butter** on **Pancakes**

by **Jonathan London**
illustrated by **G. Brian Karas**

Viking

VIKING
Published by the Penguin Group
Penguin USA, 375 Hudson Street, New York, New York 10014, U.S.A.
Penguin Books Ltd, 27 Wrights Lane, London W8 5TZ, England
Penguin Books Australia Ltd, Ringwood, Victoria, Australia
Penguin Books Canada Ltd, 10 Alcorn Avenue, Toronto, Ontario, Canada M4V 3B2
Penguin Books (N.Z.) Ltd, 182-190 Wairau Road, Auckland 10, New Zealand

Penguin Books Ltd, Registered Offices: Harmondsworth, Middlesex, England

First published in 1995 by Viking, a division of Penguin Books USA Inc.

1 3 5 7 9 10 8 6 4 2

Text copyright © Jonathan London, 1995
Illustrations copyright © G. Brian Karas, 1995
All rights reserved

LIBRARY OF CONGRESS CATALOGING-IN-PUBLICATION DATA
London, Jonathan
Like butter on pancakes / by Jonathan London;
illustrated by G. Brian Karas. p. cm.
Summary: As the sun rises and sets, its rays highlight simple
aspects and situations of farm life, including the shadow
of a cloud, the sizzle of bacon, and the dancing of spoons.
ISBN 0-670-85130-2
[1. Sun—Fiction. 2. Day—Fiction. 3. Farm life—Fiction.]
I. Karas, G. Brian, ill. II. Title.
PZ7.L8423Lg 1995 [E]—dc20 94-9154 CIP AC

Printed in Singapore
Set in Goudy Sans Black

For Michael Patrick, with a smile and a nod to Pablo Neruda — J. L.

For Cecilia Yung, from Potatoes to Pancakes — G. B. K.

Beyond the rim
of morning
the sun ticks
the birds talk

and the spoons sleep nestled
in the kitchen drawers.

First light melts
like butter on pancakes,
spreads warm and yellow
across your pillow.

A woodpecker pecks
on a lone pine.
The sun ticks
the birds talk.

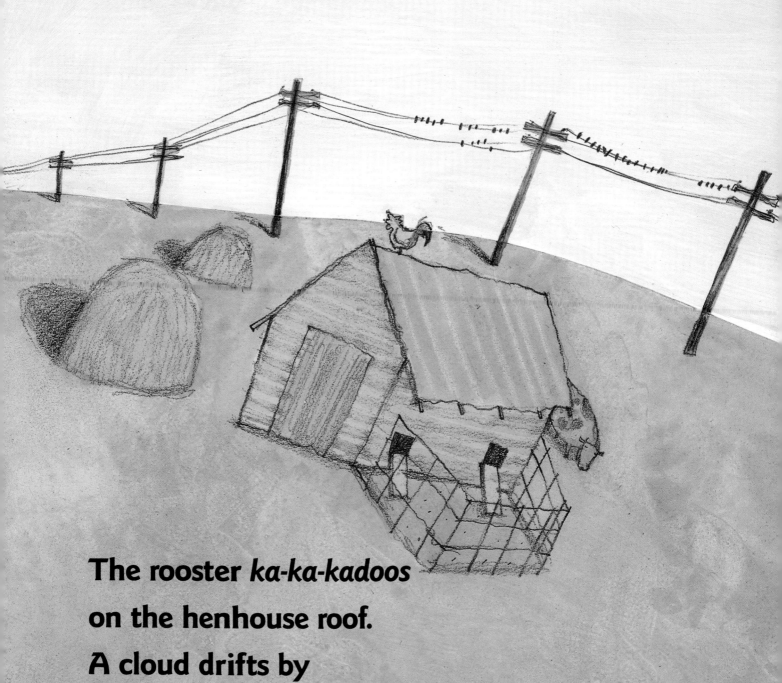

The rooster *ka-ka-kadoos*
on the henhouse roof.
A cloud drifts by
dragging a shadow.

**The sun ticks
the birds talk.
The cat purrs
rolling in the light.**

Papa's kettle whistles
Mama's bacon sizzles
slippers whisper
across the kitchen floor.

Rise 'n' shine!
Up 'n' at 'em!
Come 'n' get it!
Breakfast time!

You roll out of bed.
The smell of bacon
fills your sleepy head.
The sun ticks
the birds talk.

You pitter-patter
in your bunny slippers,
do the pajama dance
in a puddle of sun.

The spoons dance with you
the knives and forks
the cups and saucers
and all the pretty dishes.

Then you sit down to eat,
swing your feet,
pour on the syrup
and dig right in.

When you lick your milk mustache you say, "All done!"

The day has begun
and till the day is done
the sun ticks
the birds talk

**and you run and jump
and tumble in the hay.**

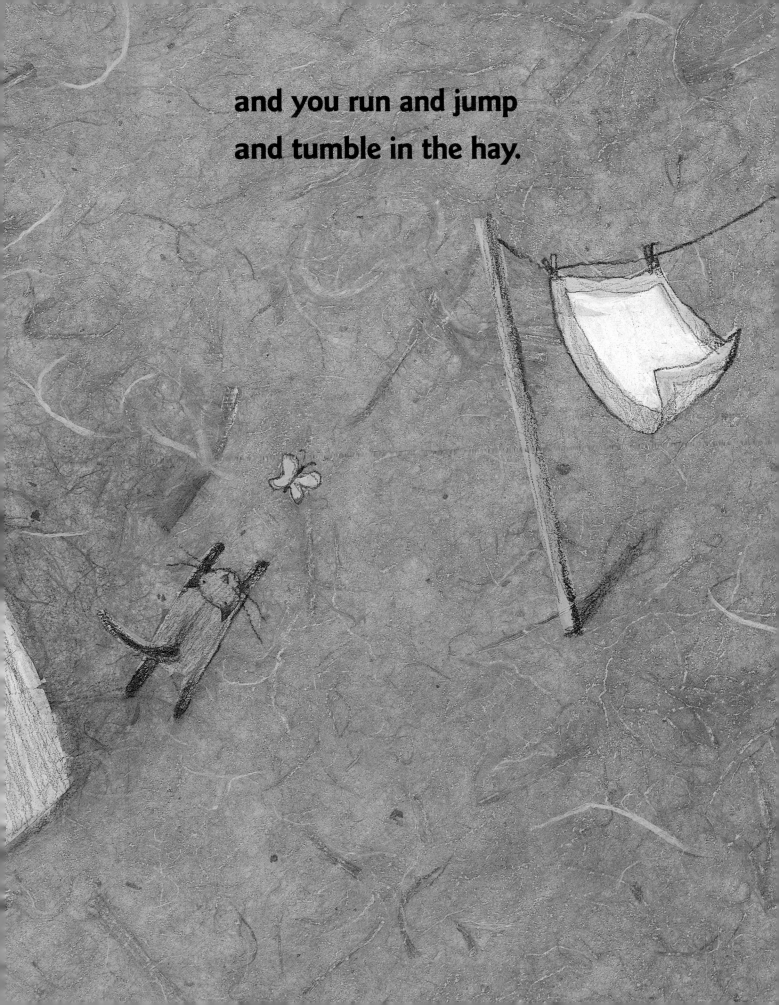

The barnyard animals
hee-haw and neigh.
They honk and they cluck
and the cow jumps over

. . . **your old red truck.**

A bell rings. Ting-a-ling!
Time to wash up!
Supper time!
Come 'n' get it!

After supper
the night creeps in
and the moon spills milk
for the cat to drink.
Mama sings
in your soft, dark room.

**Papa hums
and you drift toward dreams
on your feather pillow.**

Beyond the rim
of evening
the sun sleeps
the birds too

and the spoons sleep nestled
in the kitchen drawers.